I0407915

Mandala
Adult Coloring Book Stylish Patterns

Copyright: Published in the United States by Orville Kyle
Published January 2017
ISBN-13: 978-1542639736
ISBN-10: 1542639735

Thank you

www.ingramcontent.com/pod-product-compliance
Lightning Source LLC
Chambersburg PA
CBHW081554280526
45788CB00011B/3470